Musings
of a
MAD
SCIENTIST

Musings

of a

MAD SCIENTIST

Second Edition

David Gretch

Printed in the United States of America
ISBN 978-1-95843-481-9 (sc)
ISBN 978-1-95843-482-6 (e)

Library of Congress Control Number: 2023903422

2023.01.24

MainSpring Books
5901 W. Century Blvd
Suite 750
Los Angeles, CA, US, 90045

www.mainspringbooks.com

Table of Contents

Introduction

In publishing this second edition of *Musings of a Mad Scientist*, I have attempted three important steps related to "book hygiene". First, I needed to make the book affordable to the public. To do this required acquiring a new publishing partner, MainSpring Books. They have guaranteed me the book will be sold for an amount of about ten dollars, compared to twenty-four dollars charged by the previous publisher. Second, I have contracted with the new publisher for a marketing package that will further help make the second edition available to readers. Third, and most important, the edition has been extensively edited to trim content, smooth transitions, and make the musings more readable. I hope the book is improved and of interest to readers of this genre.

David Gretch MD, PhD
Author

To Be Human

The speed of a mind does not matter. It is only control that matters.

We are animals. Human DNA codes are related and, in some places, identical, to DNA codes of other animals. This could not be by chance. Furthermore, the very machines of life (ribosomes, mitochondria, transcription complexes, and so on) are identical among animals and humans. Most of the basic organ systems, those that support digestion, metabolism, elimination, and awareness, are also very similar among species of animals. We all live within the same energy system. We do, in fact, still possess our animal natures, but this is not the problem. Rather, our animal natures, including our appetites, are an incredible part of our being.

The problem is that we are easily manipulated, because the human animal, by nature, is trusting and gullible when it comes to higher intelligence. I have learned this about myself. I studied the rip-off machine, from its plateau, in academia, and from its dungeon, in the narrow back alleys of Portland, Oregon, for example, or in the wide avenues of our nation's capital. Under the influence of love, I was ripped off again and again; yet I was protected and allowed to witness the workings of the human soul. Not just to see how it feels, but to help me learn the lesson. I was led to the streets and protected, so I could tell a story from the streets, the best place to write from these days.

Drug addicts and alcoholics offered me company and understanding, in exchange for companionship, and occasionally money for drugs and alcohol. There were no other good choices, they said, those hard-to-imagine spirit guides, and nobody else seemed to care about what they had to say, either. Yet I cared because they clearly understood. They could understand what I was talking about. There was no easier attention to be bought than that of an addict in need. I was crazy in love, and I needed someone to talk to. I found him and her and them, impersonals, on the streets. They knew the voice of wisdom, and some of them spoke it quite well, and I recognized them because they understood me.

Warm people, cold people, warm hearts, cold hearts, sincere smiles behind crazy open brains, and disgusting, decaying bodies, in agony, with burned-out minds, yet still caring and willing to listen, or perhaps cycling between brilliance and agony, from one high to the next depth, one feeling to another, hopefully toward peace and understanding; at least they helped me along that road. Some were already there, yet they still risked death and oblivion with every shot and every drink, never fearing the fall, because of the knowledge of the loving arms (of God), faithfully awaiting every fall. They also knew the recourse of sleep, the ending and the new beginning, the miracle of life we have been blessed with. This story, written for desperate people, inspired by desperate people, is the story of our love, our connectedness, our desire to understand and help each other. We need to help the homeless people of America.

Zen Consciousness

If you can receive some of this information on the inside, then your mind will become more open to other teachings as well. Spirituality offers many, many recipes for a good life, a happy life. There are many, many beautiful self-help books out there. The universe of loving intent is reaching out to all of us with hopes of awakening our loving potential. In the end, being a loving person remains the best recipe for happiness.

Consciousness is less complex than some might realize. It is as solid as concrete, so we can approach it more easily than, say, the concepts of good and evil, which are mostly understood as ideas. Consciousness is strictly a property of the present, and consciousness is not tied to thought. It is anchored in reality, in feelings. The soul is awake.

When one is conscious (present in reality), it is a spiritual moment. This state is referred to as Zen. Zen is also referred to as a state of consciousness of God, where thought is free and glorious. Another way of viewing Zen is as a quiet understanding, or thoughtless understanding.

Besides our innate understanding of truth, kindness, and gentleness, gratitude and humility are also time-honored properties of our collective soul. When thought is fueled by love, it is good and worthy of higher consciousness, yet it needs nothing. Thoughts fueled by despair require attention because thought disorders (cognitive errors) need editing. In addition to profound intelligence of great simplicity, another property of higher consciousness is mystique or mystery. Indeed, its language is also intuition, and thus intuition is a common spiritual language of both lower and higher intelligence.

As we improve our understanding and achieve adequate quietude as a species, we will be better able to synchronize with and understand higher consciousness for what it is: another manifestation of our relationship with God. On the other hand, the wisdom of God, or Tao, exists first in the soul in quietude, then the hearts of humans, and eventually it permeates the upper realms. Although lights may flicker, the river of life runs constant and true. We are all connected through God, above and below, through His idea, love, and Her substrate, soul. God's consciousness, wisdom, Tao, is in all things, whether or not the idea of God is present.

The understanding we seek is within us. That is where we are connected. Forget heaven. Be human. Communication is nothing without understanding. Understanding is nothing without love. It is amazing what can emerge from a quiet mind (Zen).

Soul Intelligence (Simplicity)

Long before dirt hit the ground, there was mystique. We should not be afraid of our own mystical natures.

Within the pure mind (soul) are special places of profound peace, beauty, and ecstasy. It is as if it were, in fact, the very mind of God, from where we came. We are allowed in.

The soul, in the end, longs to love, and to be loved.

We are called to love.

Synchronicity

Carl Jung defined and studied parallel correlations of life's events (synchronicity) as having a subtle and mystical undertone, usually unapparent at the conscious level. Among individuals, awakening to the moment of synchronicity occurs when one recognizes the familiar within coincidence. On a nonrational basis, this occurs whenever we feel emotionally connected to other humans or other life-forms, whether the connection is good or bad, intellectual or not. My experience is that both conversation and intuition are amplified in this setting, when two or more minds share a common wavelength, at either or both the intellectual and/or emotional levels.

This is all very subtle. Surely you are helping me write this book, whether your calendar says that the year is 2015, as mine did during the first writing, 2022, as mine did during the first revision, or perhaps 2051, as yours may say. The desire for common understanding transcends time. Thank you.

Synchronicity happens every time we communicate, every time we understand each other. It also happens when we don't communicate, when we just miss it. Even if our awareness fluctuates, underneath the understanding, which may waver, our connectedness is constant, and we can still achieve the goal of successful communication. It may even come to us later, as a bolt of light perhaps. Not to worry. Just receive, digest, and be at peace. God's understanding has a life of its own, and that life will connect us and live in us if we so desire. What we are trying to achieve is awareness and simultaneous understanding of this reality, our connectedness, either in addition to, or in lieu of, shared emulsion in this conversational content.

We are working in proximity to love. How close can we get with our intellects? How much can we understand? The answer depends, surely, on our individual selves, what we have achieved regarding preparedness and reverence.

We have multiple fields of consciousness available for simultaneous experience of individual holistic perspectives. Integrating, it is apparent that this overlap reveals improved quality and depth of perception, yet knowledge is not necessary, as the search has met its destiny.

When we are awake to this reality of synchronized being, every coincidence has meaning.

Perception is allowed with understanding, and thus it is understanding that is important. Knowledge is a placeholder.

Over several decades I have conducted an unofficial study of random humans in public settings, the question being what percentage of persons at any given time appear to be spiritually connected with each other? The overall strength and significance of this type of interhuman connection seems to me to be changing (increasing) over time. I also wonder if others can detect the spiritual quickening that is among us, yet this is very difficult to study.

Based on what I have seen, you might perhaps think of one element of synchronicity as *the beat*, and other participants in synchronicity as *the dancers following the beat*. For example, on a gross scale, a subtle interpersonal energy of significant difference from the norm sometimes appears when I am around certain impersonal (egoless) persons of significant difference from the norm. Their impersonal nature does set them apart, yet it does not betray their purity of function. They are all hippies to some degree, knowledgeable and capable of free love. The Jungian concept of synchronicity allows one to imagine a mechanism whereby individual souls can move into and out of synch with other good vibration energies, and what is good for one soul is likely good for another. This seems to be working with high efficiency.

Oscillation is a scientific descriptor used to describe a type of repetitive change from a relatively grounded state (psyche) to a relatively excited state (idea) and back, with regular periodicity. It is interesting to speculate that we might be polishing the ideas as we perhaps move into and out of synch with other glorious mind-sets, for example, on a periodic basis, and yet not be aware of this fact unless we were trying to be aware, because it's so much easier if we just oscillate with the flow.

Speaking as if I were some sort of anthropologist (I am not), I have personally experienced, through sharing, an amazing spectrum of positive human mind-sets, such that I believe when it comes to the human spirit, it really is possible that we can come up with some new approaches to our old problems, something that might be benefited by awareness and understanding of our primal potentials so as to liberate our innate healing forces from the repression of our cultured selves.

Another interesting biological descriptor is "coalescence" (changing of many into one). Consciousness can do this, coalesce, and it does so periodically as well in between desolations. Soap bubbles also do this; many bubbles become one larger bubble (sometimes). With respect to synchronized overlapping consciousness, this is a beautiful and illuminating destination. Synchronized consciousness is like the blending of colors, blue and yellow into green, for example, or red and blue into purple. When the colors are separate, they are fully matured yet distinctly different. When the colors coalesce, a uniform newness results. Just as mixing bubbles and oil makes the oil soluble in water, synchronization of consciousness can help in the cleansing processes as well. Much of our healing from now on will be passive; such hard work has already been done.

Waves

Per quantum theory, whenever we are not waves, we are particles behaving in a wavelike manner to some degree or another, and per my experience, the more we slow down, the better we harmonize with our spiritual reality, so that our material and spiritual realities become closer to one, oscillating together through time, material defining the moment, the particle, and spirit defining eternity, the loving wave we oscillate in, God's essence. When we synchronize, particle with principle, together, we are truly amazing, somewhere beyond magnificent, where there is not yet a word to define the event.

The twenty-first century has become the age of coexistence of material and spiritual realities. It is not so much that the material world has awakened to the spiritual reality; more like the lightning-quick pulses of the sun's perhaps genderless rays (luminescence) have been tempered by the moon in our defense and have slowed down, elongating, to reach harmony with the bioessence (biorhythms) of Earth, so that solar intelligence and lunar intelligence have become synchronized, once again, with waves of excitement pulsating through our recent days, as if some sublime and mysterious source of direction were again breathing energy into our existence.

There is a plethora of time-honored traditions for enhancing our spirituality, which have allowed preservation of our most sacred attributes, including knowledge of our oneness with the loving maternal source (Earth) from which we have evolved. In some cultures this is not broadly disseminated knowledge, not necessarily because of traditional suppression, but out of necessity, because public dissemination of such opinion as "we all have God's internal voice within us" was branded as witchcraft, and heretics were brutally murdered in public, often by burning the bearer of opinion to the delight of public sentiment. As we (collectively the humans) become more aware and evolved in a positive direction, our understanding has increased automatically through the experience of coexistence with each other. We are learning machines. An open mind will grasp new information, just as a jellyfish struggles with its dinner during ingestion, hungry for growth. Furthermore, an open mind easily digests truth and grows exponentially. A loving mind instinctively stores truth very close to consciousness and seeks to share truths with other loving minds. A lazy mind, or hateful mind, will disregard the importance of truth and will discard it at the earliest convenience into the subconscious realms, where it won't bother anyone. Yet the subconscious realms are now exposed, so it is my hope that everyone will become infected with this new variety of truth. This new truth virus, will become a vaccine against the mind-closing power of fear, because these messages contain antifear missiles as well, heat seekers as well, and fear is only illusion. We are now fortified for the next ascent against fear (we rule hell as well) to arouse the next waves of consciousness, the next actualizations of resting moments. Can we not wake up time?

Communication is not possible without the act of mature understanding. We have to strive to see the other side of things, to "*break on through to the other side,*" as the poetry of Jim Morrison, lead singer for the sixties' rock band the Doors, first encouraged. I am not writing as a purist. I also look at alternative hypotheses, such as the one that many people have lived by for centuries: the idea of dualism, proposed early on by the Greek philosopher Plato, a former student of the sage Socrates. Of course, Plato and his contemporaries also entertained the idea of many gods (polytheism), perhaps because that was all they could understand, or perhaps back then maybe there were many gods, and He just fused into one more recently (and perhaps He can fuse and unfuse at any given moment that circumstances favor one or the other state of Being).

If we stay with the moment, it is true: reality and thought can synchronize, and truth can be experienced. If one (truth or thought) should be discarded, it should be thought, unless one needs to escape from reality, and then thought might be the best avenue available to us to escape into at that moment. A pessimist might perhaps conclude that thought evolved to help us escape from dismal reality. We might enjoy freeing ourselves from the imprisonment (of reality), as pursued in our youth, and perhaps rely more heavily on the relatively quiet voice of wisdom.

With respect to the discerning mind today, compared to antiquity, we potentially might understand spirituality, if not intelligence, better because of the physics of quantum mechanics pursued by the intellect and gestalt of Einstein and the logic of deductive reasoning initially championed by Aristotle and later purified by the teachings of various sages, including Jiddah Krishnamurti, who taught the deviance and mastery of thought in his works, including the classic books *Freedom from the Known* and *The Flame of Attention.*

We no longer need to fear. We have had good reason in the past to be afraid. If our lives are poisoned by toxic ideas, it is because of our own error or error of the establishment, which has abused us (perhaps) even more than we have abused ourselves. Fear has taught us to hate each other. Since we need to face the source of our fear before we overcome it, I'll just tell you that it is economic, and we will discuss this further later.

To Listen

Fear is like glue that keeps false ideas stuck in the mind. Exposing fear and letting go of false ideas unveils truth.

- David Gretch

* * *

The ability to observe without evaluating is the highest form of intelligence.

- Jidda Krishnamurti

* * *

What lies behind us and what lies ahead of us are tiny matters compared to what lives within us.

- Henry David Thoreau

Thinking can be a drug. It can put us to sleep. Yet it is only a sub-portion of our mind that needs to think. The rest listens. The listening part, the observing part, the reading part, that which listens to us think or ignores us as we think or plays the piano as we think, which can focus and sustain thought, as well as ignore it or partially ignore it, that is to say, look at a thought or thought train, perhaps, using peripheral vision, is what I choose to call our critical thinking apparatus; it is very subtle, yet I find it the most interesting aspect of our minds. It is related to deep thinking; it is sticky like glue (holds thoughts tightly if needed) and feels as if "I am." The deeper the thought, the tighter the focus, the more the thinking apparatus becomes disengaged from other reality. If you understand this message, you are undoubtedly using your critical thinking apparatus.

Critical thinking, considering all perspectives fairly, is a great thing. Practice of critical thinking can cure thought disorders in more ways than one. First, it provides new information, for critical thinking, by my definition, is searching for the purpose of accumulation of information. It is not necessarily being negative of something, some point of view. Although critical thinking resists emotional bias, the critical thinker can be ecstatic with emotion upon discovery, for example. Yet critical thinking can also be extremely dense, extremely slow, and extremely difficult. I learned how arduous human logic is by reviewing and critiquing large numbers of scientific grant proposals for competitive funding by the National Institutes of Health. With practice, the highly focused mind can learn to relax and function better, even despite distractions, once evolved to maturity.

Focused attention on breath control leads to conscious rejuvenation of the critical thinking apparatus. It is here that we can examine thoughts with our peripheral vision while focusing on breath. We can learn to distinguish our critical thinking from the background mental noise that may have resulted from previous mind conditioning, or early childhood trauma, for example. We can learn to control our breath and observe our thoughts with our critical thinking apparatus, coming and going, to become more familiar with them and the emotions they might tend to associate with.

As we do this, what we are focusing is our critical thinking apparatus, under our own auspices. No one else is in control. Sometimes a quiet mind results, in which thinking is sharp and exact. In contrast, a restless mind may remain active in many directions, and the observer initially finds focus impossible and effort highly uncomfortable. Yet this is an important aspect of the mind, this observation of restless thinking, looking for purpose, and even the intention to pay attention to the mind is important progress. My performance as a medical scientist improved soon after I began to observe my mind with my mind.

In my humble experience, yes, a rapidly responsive mind is highly desirable. When a studious mind refocuses abruptly, analytical perspectives merge. Since my critical thinking machine was trained by many influences, including schools, universities, societies, churches, temples, and so on, some of which represented vastly differing perspectives, it lives with the fact of multiple distinct data fields. Keeping an open mind means not jumping to conclusions. When we focus our critical thinking, we can remember with acuity amazing things.

In summary, critical thinking is good for the mind, even when it resembles struggle, in my opinion. In the end, critical thinking becomes listening to silence, and breath. True listening, in silence, is freedom.

Sweet Emotions

Our inner realms are connected by universal energy which flows through us at emotional frequencies too slow for normal detection, yet brilliant when detected during meditation. We may or may not be aware of this. Emotions are fountains of our soul, and we are connected through these fountains. As soulful sweet emotions boil over, love trickles down through our personal lives. What becomes distilled is a common desire for fairness, adding momentum to the loving transformation of mankind.

By extrapolation from the leading theories of evolution, I believe emotion preceded thought from a phylogenetic perspective. The implication is that emotional intelligence was our first form of intelligence, and it is possible that it is also our most mature, enlightened form of intelligence as well.

Monkeys have powerful emotions, but limited intellectual capacity compared to humans. Thought, as a survival advantage, and then as an evolutionary force, allowed us to take control of our lives, or allowed someone else to take control of our lives, and our environments, and now it will hopefully help us learn about all of this survival of the fittest. It is a bit dangerous. Thought seems to fear emotion, seems innately better than emotion, perhaps because emotion knows that thought is a common source of fear, even though emotions are blamed for fear, and as such, thought is the only thing to fear. Jean-Paul Sartre, remember, defined the soul as "all that has resulted from the desire to think." Perhaps so, for him, but for me, the desire to love defines my soul, and it is quite possible that this intelligent desire to love came first, before thought, and even before the desire to think. That's what makes emotional language such a tricky language. It is comprised mostly of silence.

I also think my loving soul mates will probably be happy to think about this love and its desire to grow and to be shared through the windows of free will, for I believe in this writing on behalf of the soul, this human soul that longs to love. This love has consciousness, is conscious, and seeks to live, to express, and to be received, and it has been received and shared and is satisfied—for the moment. Crazy thing about this love is that it needs forever.

It is very interesting to me that memory and emotion are housed together in the oldest part of the brain. Intelligence, or cognitive ability as it is otherwise called, is housed in the newer part of the brain. It is my opinion that the function of this newer part of the brain, ironically, is to protect the older stuff, such as innate intuition, our thoughtless knowing. Know your feelings and defend them if needed.

The importance of emotion in learning has been vastly underestimated by our culture, in my humble opinion. I am not really trained as an educator, so please think of this as another of my philosophies. Collectively, as spirits, we are still an adolescent society, if not juvenile, but certainly not yet mature. Our thoughts are complex beyond description and even imagination. Our feelings are active, hyperactive, and repressed; our creativity is dynamite and repressed. Collectively, we are exuberant and frustrated, and some are frightened. Yet much beauty and brilliance have persisted; God's grace has grown.

The Beat Goes On

Life becomes more beautiful, the slower you go, as if beauty matures only during time's decelerations, as if the blossoming of beauty takes time, one way or another, yet the only difference is that our ability to perceive is enhanced as we take our time. Do not rush hastily away from beauty.

Whereas the peace train is difficult to attain and perhaps more difficult to maintain, it is as easy as honking your horn in traffic to create conflict. Hate is like fire once it is created (even if out of nothing). As exploiters continue to use devious approaches to drive your fear, and our foreign policy, for as long as they can, do not be discouraged. The situation will resolve itself once the vendors of hate are exposed before the public eye and we realize that we really don't hate (fear) each other as much as we once thought we did—certainly not as much as they told us to do.

The fact that ego can overcome decadent spirit or wayward logic and mount an honorable and even blessed life was aptly portrayed many centuries ago by Saint Augustine, and many subsequent mystics, just as I am certain that many of us have been chosen by God to do His work in this present day and age.

I am finally starting to get a handle on the phenomenon of impersonal life, how God is making personal (human) appearances in life whenever He likes. It all started about the time that the devastating earthquake hit Haiti, shortly after Katrina bathed New Orleans, and right before the Gulf of Mexico oil spill. All of that activity suggested that Father Sky had come down to Earth for a spell, and the evidence suggests His home base was somewhere around the southeastern portion of the United States (or Mexico); yet He is mystical, so He could potentially show up anywhere.

The mystical aspect all started making sense when I expanded my fascination with our nation's love-drenched hippie culture and looked deeper into the message of the generation that inspired the hippies, the *beat generation*. Ironically banned by the Catholic Church and initially censored by court action, the *beat authors and poets* spoke with inspired voices, and despite their refusal to ignore the blatant decadence in our society (a bold author named Ernest Hemmingway also illuminated this from Europe a generation earlier), a lot of people really loved their stuff! Yet many couldn't understand the message, much as many might not understand the mystery of the Blessed Trinity, for example. It wasn't necessarily the writers' shortfall. The message was clear: God is in and among us, in Spirit, in everything, every day, working for the same lofty goals we all crave, only in some cases, God is perhaps having more fun than we are. I truly believe the *beat authors and poets* knew they were playing with God's stuff, as if He had leaked it out over the times (late 1940s and early 1950s) to help prepare us for the shocking sixties. Even in my own imagination, when I park my own runaway thought train, it seems to me as if *that same beat still goes on*. Can you let me know if it passed your depot?

Mystical experience is different from religion. It is a type of communication between God and man or God and woman, where God reveals a part of His Sacred to the mystic, and the mystic expresses the love and radiance as best possible, with the Grace of God as help. Mystical writing implies that God is helping. Aldous Huxley wrote a masterful summary of mystical writings in his book titled *The Perennial Philosophy*. His deep understanding is evident from a simple quote gathered from the book's introduction:

Reality is such that it cannot be directly and immediately apprehended except by those who have chosen to fulfil certain conditions, making themselves loving, pure in heart, and poor in spirit. Why should this be so? We do not know. [1]

It is very difficult to understand this, and perhaps the more intelligent we are, the harder it is for us to be humble. C. S. Lewis, an Irish mystic / former atheist educated at Oxford, was made a fellow at both Magdalen College and Cambridge University. He was indeed a very

---

[1]   Aldous Huxley *The Perennial Philosophy* (Harper and Brothers: New York, 1945), viii

famous writer of children's books (the *Narnia* series), and he was also a famous Christian author (e.g. *Mere Christianity*). It is possible that thinking like a child helped convert Lewis. A minor tenet of Christianity is to be childlike in our approach to God. Children are great learners and initially fearless, and children have great access to knowledge of God because their minds are uncrowded.

According to Leonard Shlain, author of *The Alphabet Versus the Goddess*, as we become educated, some of us lose our ability to know God because we acquire apparently contradictory evidence, or commit neuronal circuitry to other grand ideas, such as science. Still, many of us continue to have faith, even though it might be impossible to imagine what God is like. And once we quit imagining, and start experiencing, it becomes easier, I think.

Whereas C. S. Lewis publicly refused to speculate on God's female side, Mother Universe, or Grand Mother Earth, or Mother Nature, because the intellectual environment could not allow resolution of the disturbance such consideration would certainly arouse, I do call attention to Her, and I do hope this will also attract considerable attention. I assume in my writing that the time is ripe for such consideration, and all will either welcome this, much as they did a lunar eclipse on the harvest supermoon of September 2015, or they already knew about Her and the tender love She imparts on all creation, only this love starts at ground zero, the center of

Earth, Her womb, and everything revolves around Her and us—once again, mystically, of course.

On many occasions of social conversation, I have found it quite amazing how aware people are of God's Wisdom. They are not surprised by our recent progress, just as they weren't surprised by the plethora of issues that has continuously stagnated and frustrated our journey toward integration and fulfillment as an intelligent species. They exist in, but do not profit from, this stagnation. They have been patient if nothing else. Therefore, for their benefit, I present an agenda that would also assault the tremendous apathy and social entrenchment from which we collectively suffer, so that the solvable global problems of starvation and illiteracy can be properly addressed. I have come to believe that, in contrast to hating the cause(s) of this injustice, we must love and understand our brothers and sisters who have been enslaved on the paths laid down by the unjust, so they will hasten to our aid in the battle for the liberation of all oppressed peoples. Let us together drop our weapons, feed the entire planet, house the homeless, and treat the sick. Come on humanity, we can do this!

A Natural Matter

Americans, like human beings everywhere, believe many things that are obviously untrue . . . Their most destructive untruth is that it is very easy for any American to make money. They will not acknowledge how in fact hard money is to come by, and, therefore, those who have no money blame and blame and blame themselves. This inward blame has been a treasure for the rich and powerful, who have had to do less for their poor, publically and privately, than any other ruling class since, say, Napoleonic times.[2]

—Kurt Vonnegut

Mother Earth (Gaia) is alive, fire in Her belly, life sprouting on Her shell. She is the real world. We are not much more than Her normal flora. Let's not be toxic parasites.

When life gets difficult, I often seek sanctity through connection with Nature, including non-human forms of creation, and even rock can be a place to focus and remember reverence. The living universe, on Earth, is a source of profound understanding. The soul is emotional. Wisdom, patience, resilience, kindness, and empathy are soulful characteristics. I believe every human shares the same soul beatitude, if cultivated. That means, if every human were educated as to the beauty and delicate balance of nature, there might not be any pollution and global warming, glacial decay and extinction of noble species. Today, for a subset of people, monetary profit is more important than long term survival of the planet. Through education, we might be able to reverse this horrific trend.

Furthermore, from a humanistic perspective, there is no reason some humans should be allowed to accumulate vast excesses of wealth, while others starve, homeless on the streets. Many children starve every day. Excess profits of the ultra-wealthy would fit nicely into social programs. Excess wealth could also be used to battle adverse environmental impact. In my opinion, deeply punitive monetary penalties should be imposed on corporations violating environmental standards, and the practice of profiting off pollution must stop. Pollution must be stopped.

I have seen evidence of God, and others have as well, and it seems to me that this suffering and destruction we are into might be a periodic phenomenon. Yet it does feel to me as if the beat is still ongoing, that love is growing and that the future is brighter than we can imagine.

Mother Earth is a love-generating planet, and many humans are love generators. Love generators growing on a love generator; there must be something in Her water, although the importance of this has been vastly underestimated throughout our history.

Sometimes it seems as if God has evolved into what we have allowed Him to become . . . nothing in the minds of some large proportion of humans, and everything in the minds of some believers. Possibly God also exists as something in between and extending beyond these boundaries. God is leading us. Love is leading us. How can we prove this? Again, perhaps the in-between is possible, that at some points in history, perhaps God has allowed us to guide the direction of our collective fate(s), while other times He has led.

It is very scientific to assume that earthlings evolved from Earth, instead of that outer space DNA seeding theory that is rather difficult to argue against without evidence. Conglomerate views of love evolving on Earth, intimately connected with eternity through a mere shift in frame of reference, will hopefully emerge as left-brain intelligence loosens up a bit in order to better understand reality beyond thought.

Human intelligence can at least understand the power of a shift in perspective by noting the tremendous flexibility of our respective individual imaginations over the course of history, including multiple perspectives from abundant unique languages. This flexibility should encourage us to hope that someday we will have the capability to understand well beyond our present status, to overcome our toxic idea structure that manifests as survival of the fittest, and an unfair playing board with blatant disregard for toxic impact on our environment including earth and water, fish, animals, birds, and other humans.

Contrary to the way things might appear from time to time, human nature, in its primal and innocent stage, Is gentle and kind, and I am not always mad. I have observed such bliss as gentle kindness thriving within some, but not all, of the days I have examined thus far, ever since I learned the true and unique beauty of gentle kindness, which, to my senses, is akin only to reverent silence in its calming effects. Yes, we are earthlings, and yes, I believe earthlings are spirit beings. We evolved right here on the shell of Mother Earth, a byproduct of Nature, and we have survived; this is earth love, love generated on earth, magical and medicinal and mystical love.

To summarize, I believe we are either love generators, love enhancers, love entrepreneurs, or unique combinations of the three. Having generated ripples in life, inspiring understanding and loving action, we continue on despite exploitation and oppression, and one day, we shall overcome.

Earth Rhythms

More sublime than I can describe, akin to the music of butterflies, unrecognized, forceful, guiding evolution from time to time throughout history, I suspect, is Earth consciousness. Scientists would be become thrilled to know Her better if they could acquire the required reverence. One needs highly sensitive feelings in order to truly understand this love frequency.

I believe strongly that every time we expose conflict and then resolve it, we gain new ground for positivity to expand into. That's the tilling portion of the work, the other being seed planting (planting of good ideas).

As rock legend Bob Dylan said, "The times they are a-changin'." Only this time it's different. Time is not so much slipping into the future, as before. Now, much more, time is slowing down and expanding into the present, letting the past catch up (if it wants). If you happen to observe the slowdown, or if you perhaps perpetually live in the slowdown, you will know what I'm talking about.

I buffer my coffee with vanilla, a form of aromatherapy. I theorize that since the beginning, Mother Earth has been alive, and She is now the same low-frequency conscious love energy entity as our soul; she is indeed the Mother of our soul, we humans, and furthermore, we evolved from Her, on Her, in Her. Mother Earth, and Grandmother Earth.

Only by intense examination can I understand meaning, its purpose, before it will be quiet. In my estimate there are two worlds: the thought world, and the world that is thought about. The two worlds can merge with understanding, if only for a moment, yet sometimes they are vastly different. The word of thought, in constructive imagination, for example, can be used to improve the world we think about. The problem's solution lies in what we do with thought. What are our priorities? How do we harness the best? That should be our goal.

Because of our unique individual perspective comes the unavoidable fact that no person can assume all perspectives. One would have to experience every life, learn every lesson, every success, and every failure. Thus, there is more to reality than we can recognize through conventional thought. Just as understanding grows in accordance with our attention span, bushes that are watered faithfully during hot summer nights will continue to show their blossoms proudly into the Autumn season.

One might think like a lot of other people that what we need to further reform is the human ego, yet I do not believe it is all that simple. Ego is a part of individual development, and what we need for consensus understanding of peace are healthy, compassionate egos.

I suspect that healthy egos will develop spontaneously with proper nurturing. When it comes down to the truth of the matter, every single unique perspective is not only valid; it must be embraced so that it can be better expressed and understood.

For example, highly intelligent people fight to deny the existence of God. It is sometimes worthwhile to look at their arguments. Skeptics will always be among us, encouraging us to open our minds in other directions, away from the dogma we were taught. Richard Dawkins, a respected biologist from Oxford, is an intellectual leader in the anti-God movement (trendy in science these days), and his book *The God Delusion* has already reached many million readers. Dawkins claims lack of evidence for God as evidence that God does not exist. Unfortunately, there is a very simple rule that lack of evidence is not itself evidence. Richard Dawkins has no data to support his argument that God is a delusion. It is merely what he believes, based on his life experiences. I am also a scientist. Based on my life experiences, I have overwhelming evidence that God exists. I am just one data point; there are many, many more. God is everywhere I have looked. Why are some minds unable to see what is so brilliant to others? It may be deviant mis-trained ego that keeps us from seeing beauty, I don't know.

In his widely embraced book entitled *Man's Search for Meaning*, Viktor E. Frankl, a psychiatrist and Nazi concentration camp survivor, reveals the perspective that modern man exists in an existential vacuum, which, in my opinion, recalls the effects of mass hypnosis:

No instinct tells him what he has to do, and no tradition tells him what he ought to do; sometimes he does not even know what he wishes to do. Instead, he either wishes to do what other people do (conformism) or he does what other people wish him to do (totalitarianism). [3]

However, it is refreshing to realize that this bleak perspective is overcome whenever man identifies and pursues a significant (loving) goal. Once the giving of love occupies our consciousness, the existential vacuum is occupied by love, and we become free from the grinding effects of social programming and its conformity to mediocrity.

As a final point to this Chapter, the scientist I am is proud to be related to animals, birds, and even, albeit to a lesser degree, fish, reptiles, amphibians, plants and insects. I love life here on the Earth plane. I believe we should all respect (and care for) other life on our beautiful planet. This consciousness alone cures the existential vacuum.

---

[3]   Viktor E. Frankl *Man's Search for Meaning* (Boston: Beacon Press, 1959), 106

Thoughts on Memory

From my perspective, memory is more than a storage bank; it seems to have an intellectual life of its own. Repressed memory intuitively results in repressed consciousness. That is one reason why memory is important—because it supports consciousness. Yet my gut feeling is that memory can repress consciousness when what is needed is numbness. Mechanics take over and can walk us around the playground, so to speak, of our intellectual values. Memory is our friend and asset. It can allow us to organize, create and live abundant lives, with or without concern for the suffering of others. On top of memory, guiding its expression, if we allow, a conscience will evolve. If we pay careful attention to our memories, carefully nurturing those memories that best support happiness, we will learn the bliss of service to others, the joy of helping. Furthermore, it seems logical to assume that imagination is supported by memory.

Conflicts are a part of life in our advanced society. It is comforting and liberating of thought when we have resolved the conflicts that would otherwise crowd and distort our subconscious. Repressed conflict is commonplace in our semi-abusive society, and against this we remain quietly angry. Because of social rules, we act within historically established rules of conduct, so perhaps we don't remember as much as we could these days because so much of it, the compromise and all, we cannot forget. Although we try to leave conflict behind us, to hopefully make room for positive emotions, our subconscious is and ultimately, conscience, is geared for honesty and truth. Sometimes pursuit of truth requires conflict.

By resolving conflict, we might restore memory, and reduce anger. If all we do is remember the smiles, dwelling on the positivity, then we will all smile more, and eventually, the frustration will dissipate as well. If we consciously oppose our brainwashing, we will gain clarity and pride.

Perhaps you've heard of the phantom limb phenomenon? I heard of it firsthand from a one-legged Vietnam veteran in downtown Seattle. His injury was real, his pain was real, but his limb wasn't. He had lost it to a land mine. To him, the pain was originating from his limb. But his limb was gone. There was no way for this brave and intelligent man to change this fact. My suspicion, or should I say deduction, is that memory is more powerful than even our strongest logic combined with our greatest courage. Vietnam vets went through hell for us. We need to remember and help them.

Awareness oscillates between consciousness and the collective unconsciousness, as others have called the spirit world. It is good to be aware that spirituality is in fact shared space to the extent that it is now fully synchronized with our material world, which means that all of our problems are now spiritual, that dualism is only a separating idea, and that egos are useful tools for doing spiritual work.

When our subconscious has been cleared, we can travel along a path of healthy memories. Our souls hopefully progress to enhanced awareness and experience of the fullest range of human emotions, from peace to glory and back again, as if God or heaven were shining a light for us. One aspect of the beauty of Indigenous societies lies in their cultural abilities to nurture authentic selves from birth through adulthood via the use of traditions such as song and story, art and dance. Out of reverence for our historical peoples still surviving on Earth, it would be good if we could redirect the growth of our common global human society back to a place where everyone is equal, all life is related, and all have reverence and opportunity to share our individual and collective gifts.

One Reality

Not everything that closes our mind separates us. Some protect us. Inner light easily dissolves toxic ideas. Once the toxic ideas are dissolved, better ideas can either wake up, or the mind can become seeded by new thoughts and new ideas. As a result, it becomes harder to remember the bad influence, and the desire to do so is weaker. Forgetting the bad influence is a good surrogate for forgiveness. Forgiveness is the elixir of freedom.

A quiet portion of our mind deserves credit for orchestrating this spiritual proximity and shared understanding. Perhaps the more different our paths and the more foreign our ego thoughts are to each other, the more we have to offer each other if we can overcome our vulnerabilities. I believe in the idea that as you grow, we grow. What I gain from connecting with you I may never know, but I will grow if you grow, because all growth is connected, interdependent, self-balancing, forgiving, enriching, and rewarding. I hope we collectively can grow in our trust, understanding, and loving service, and away from selfishness, fear, and apathy of our more adolescent condition.

It is my present hypothesis that there is only *one* reality, although *it* is of mystical nature and therefore *it* appears differently to everyone, of course, since we all have unique perspectives. Even the animals, fish, trees, and birds each have a unique perspective; the extent to which they perhaps contribute to overall understanding is a mystery. Yet, I strongly suspect they all have their own unique intelligence, each with their own types of thoughts. This belief is derived from communication experiments I conducted. I also suspect that different humans have different types of thoughts that convey information in a manner not yet recognized by psychologists as subtle variations in intelligence (for example, some think like fish; others like birds or specific animals).

Many people I have met in passing claim they can understand animals, while fewer understand birds and oh so few understand fish. Perhaps everyone could understand nature language at an earlier stage in our development if appropriate reverence were cultivated in this regard, as is the case with Native Americans for example. My belief is that modern culture has buried primal language skills under the dogmas and beliefs of civilization. It is also my belief that we humans share common, primordial thoughts and other common ways of thinking, in the subconscious realm for most, and conscious realm for others.

I believe every life, every consciousness, has a unique perspective. An energy (which feels to me like God's pulse) permeates interplanetary space and apparently extends to the ends of the universe (scientists previously believed this was a vacuum). The energy is now measurable. Philosophically, the energy appears to order reality (otherwise there would be naught but chaos), and we consider this ordering property to have purpose, such as justice and equanimity. Regarding what this connecting energy might be, the Seattle musician Jimi Hendrix believed that experience is ultimately what we need. Jimi played righteous guitar as he tenderly sang "The Wind Cries Mary" and understood, no doubt in my mind, the humble virtues of our Blessed Mother, and I can feel Her Love in my heart as well. The intelligence of Her Love is amazing! Maybe we all have different sensitivities, but it's my guess that She puts it all out there for each and every one of us, every day, know it or not.

I apologize for my digressions. Back to the idea of one reality. Ideas may have something to do with the problem of our apparent separateness, and the solution. As old ideas meet new ideas, or vice versa, when we are discussing topics such as God and holiness, good and evil, there can be very real contradictions. When I stopped to consider various issues, from multiple different perspectives, I realized that some contradiction is expected because, as perspectives differ, opposing perspectives are bound to occur as vision expands. Only when I recognized the necessity of contradiction could the contradiction be resolved, and enhanced learning could proceed. Most importantly, a threat-free environment helps me drop historical idea defenses so that complex learning can occur. As a population dealing with reformation of idea structure for the purpose of bettering humanity, once we free up longstanding cultural ideas from their logical or pathological structure (bad ideas parasitizing good ideas) and allow idea competition to occur, then bad ideas can eventually be put to rest, and downtrodden old good ideas can be restored and rejuvenated.

Other than that idea about idea competition, I really don't have much more to offer other than smiling: an act of kindness, a key to love.

The Mind World

I believe it must be a highly important defining quality of our interpersonal destination, the desire to communicate about such grand topics as being human, having an ego, being a spirit, having (or being) a soul, and having (or being) a voice of the soul (emotion), or even being of the nature that one is capable of hearing such a subtle voice. I'm not talking about common understanding; I'm talking about "time is an illusion" spiritual understanding. I hope we can get there. Perhaps you are there. There are always multiple conversations; I often remind myself of that fact. When faced with confusion, just slow down; something exciting is often around the corner.

Devoted and reverent thought, conditioned by years of prayer and meditation, is very slow to venture away from the sanctity of truth. Since we take ourselves with us wherever we go, as we travel around God's mind (one way of looking at it), we should remember to be open to whatever glory He and She wish to share with us, for He cannot give us anything we do not long to receive, and She never asks for credit for what She continuously gives us, whether we ask and thank Her, or not. It is not as if Her understanding (Wisdom) is even more magnificent than His; we just receive (intuition) more naturally from Her, without even thinking. At times we get stuck, no doubt, because of fear of offending Him or Her. Having faced a veritable abundance of fear (much instilled by society) and to avoid confusion, we just need to know that They are loving parents. Perhaps rules and discipline make it easier to focus on Their essence. That would explain the popularity of religion. Their diversity might explain why we have so many religious options. Rather than anything else, however, for some, including myself, it is relaxing acceptance that makes it easier for us to allow Their Love into our daily lives. Each religion is a valid path to holiness.

More Thoughts on Mind

Some ideas are toxic to others. So are some plants, such as deadly nightshade. We have a mystical cure for deadly nightshade. What you put in a mind regulates what types of ideas and beliefs can grow or not grow. A mind with bad ideas may not want to grow at all. Although fresh ideas can revive a tired mind and stimulate a new growth atmosphere, one really needs love, as well, to kill the toxic deadly nightshade. During this revival process, bad old thoughts need to be squashed, just as a farmer pulls out the weeds as faithfully as he waters and fertilizes. Squash your own bad thoughts. You have the power. Use your own love. Enjoy yourselves. You are not alone.

The mind is also a place for good ideas to rest when not in use. In fact, all ideas can exert various degrees of positive or negative influence over how the mind perceives information, especially when the mind is tired. As good ideas rest, they listen, especially when the mind is trying to grow, when the mind is listening as well.

Repetitive sound energy is an automatic cleaning apparatus of the mind. It can help new ideas grow in the mind that is tired, confused, or resistant for some other reason.

The mind is an aspect of our individual being that can open or close, much like a flower on a plant. It does a lot of our automatic thinking for us. A clean mind, free of illusion, absorbs and stores endless information at conscious, subconscious (emotional), and unconscious (spiritual) levels. The mind is also directly involved in memory recall. The trained mind can understand the intelligence of birds, animals, and emotions. The mind can listen, coordinate thought, and weigh in on matters of deep concern, much as the heart weighs in on affairs involving love.

One opinion states that the human mind is a gift from God to house our sacred consciousness as we travel through life, alongside God, into infinity and timelessness, beyond tamer imagination if we choose. When there is love, heart and soul are one. There is no need for thought. We know truth via our sixth sense, intuition, our mind's eye.

The Machine Mind

Culture has both its advantages and its disadvantages. *Machine mind* is a term used to describe the mechanics behind modern cultural programming, and it is not necessarily a bad thing. I do need to emphasize that point, for I have often thought of it as outrageously bad, always bad. It is programming of our animus, our ancient reptilian mind, and I suspect it is the same mental mechanism that Egyptian pharaohs brainwashed (perhaps using reptilian energetics for mass hypnotization) to get the pyramids built. Call it group subliminal conditioning.

Reptiles can be quite content sitting around, doing nothing, and have lots of mental clarity. I have a bona fide reptilian mind, and I have observed the mechanics of many an insect mind as well, of both the lower (e.g., ants) and higher (e.g., butterflies) chakra variety. The pharaohs may have had the formula of how to get the people to love them enough so that anything was possible. Justice was only in her infancy, so we need not look to the Egyptians for understanding of justice. However, I have begun to suspect that the wisdom of ancient Egypt might be able to help us understand the injustice we live in throughout our present-day society, why we have such mindless social advancement toward material destinies, which I believe is the most repulsive realization in the human soul at present.

I wonder if it would shake up the machine mind to hike to a pristine waterfall and observe the healing vibrancy of Nature up close. It was in the presence of unspeakable silence that I watched wave after wave of brilliantly colored butterflies, oranges and yellows and whites and blues, play in the sun's rays, hopping from flower to flower, madly, for what seemed like hours, whole clouds of them, and *the beat was there, indeed.*

We should also be aware of positive potentials of the machine mind, such as a call to civil duty, religious stewardship, and the gravitation toward increased complexity of learning provided by information technology. It is noteworthy that the machine mind has several common programs, besides just buy the latest and greatest stuff, avoid overexertion, hurry up and guard what you have or hurry up and get in line, make your point, and get to the end of the sentence. *Machine mind can also sniff out lies,* and thus may have a conscience. In theory, machine mind might be able to overcome conversion of our desires toward healthy food and exercise and can help guide us towards social justice. Harnessing this aspect of our group psychology is therefore a most desirous destination.

By harnessing the machine mind, one might hope to inspire awareness of a different, quieter, yet distinctly modern cultural revolution in America. In my mind, this is the blossoming of the Age of Aquarius, and it is all good, and it will only get better. The brilliance of the small children is all one needs to offer as evidence that the spirit of Beauty is alive and well in America. Fortunately, much of such tender spirit has been protected from adverse machine mind programming by the deemphasizing of media influence secondary to better communication (the Internet). Hopefully, educational reform will manifest as soon as it becomes more painfully obvious what a poor job we are doing in our nation's schools. Educational reform might be looked at as an attempt to adjust our machine mind paradigm away from materialistic apathy, towards righteousness and justice.

Some view machine mind characteristics as despicable. This descriptor of mindless society is not new:

> . . . machine men, with machine minds and machine hearts! You are not machines, you are not cattle, you are men! You have the love of humanity in your hearts. You don't hate: only the unloved hate, the unloved and the unnatural. Soldiers, don't fight for slavery, fight for liberty! You the people have the power, the power to create machines, the power to create happiness! You the people have the power to make this life free and beautiful, to make this life a

wonderful [4]adventure! Then, in the name of democracy, let us use that power. Let us all unite! Let us fight for a new world, a decent world . . .

—Charles Chaplin[3]

Selfish corporations, such as those that build oil pipelines under critical water sources (for profit), need to be brought under control before they ruin our precious rivers. No amount of money can repair a damaged river polluted by oil and fracking debris. Yes, our country has plenty of resources, plenty of ingenuity, plenty of wealth. However, we urgently need to regain control over the health management of our natural resources. Social revolution means revolution in our buying habits (society is economy). Many people lack hope, or are indifferent to the present situation. Where does the numbness come from? It seems to me to be forced on us without us knowing, as part of the act of consuming. Yet, freeing up the machine mind might not be that difficult. There is a way to de-pollute the mind, and once that is done, a clarification of understanding can occur. In fact, this is happening, as the Internet is continuously exposing false truths with high efficiency. If we put social reconstruction as the main agenda for the machine mind (by individual approval, for example), then the virtuous flexibility of

---

[4]   Charles Chaplin *The Great Dictator* (British Board of Film Classification: 1940)

the machine will become evident as never before. The situation is definitely fixable, just like changing the air filter on a dirty lawn mower or furnace. Alter the programming, and the mind-set will improve.

I have wondered how the machine mind came to be, and whose idea was, this cultural programming. Perhaps it just evolved, and we just need to understand it, as it may have been very important for more than only driving consumerism. Were any soldiers brainwashed to kill the enemy to survive? Does military have innate expertise at machine mind programming? Our defense instincts are intense, perhaps insect-like in maneuvers of aggression.

A common opinion is that war is good for the economy, and hate is essential to commit the country to ongoing aggression and war. We must not hold opinion against the soldiers, for they are our protectors. They act in the only manner possible, considering the situation and their sense of duty. We need to hold the establishment, the attitude of entitlement to a violent government, responsible, not ourselves nor our military. Our military is not the establishment. The establishment (exploiters and their media) may have temporary control over the level of conflict, perhaps. However, the situation is definitely fixable, and it is good to know that the establishment does not control the military.

War is not only profitable for arms dealers and oil corporations, it is also a diversion that keeps society preoccupied so they overlook problems such as corporate extraction and pollution of our countries natural resources. Communication is needed. The internet will hopefully help us to put the violent and exploitative mind-set behind us and return justice to our nation.

In my ideal society, we would all undergo love training of our egos (via poetry), and we would all be nonviolent.

We are led by leaders that are noble, corrupt or neutral. Thus, when our societies appear to be either noble or corrupt, we must keep in mind that society is usually a reflection of the leadership. Much of the pattern was laid down in the past, when we were undereducated, and what we have now is nothing more than a misdirected partially educated society. I would imagine that changing habits is much easier for an educated society than for an uneducated society, especially now that mass communication is efficient and apparently unrestricted.

Higher Education of the Ego

Higher education should not be inflation of the ego. Inflated ego can kill intuition. I suspect that institutions differ with respect to the value they put upon intuition, based on the amount of ego required to maintain their definitions of success. Intuitive people know they are intuitive unless somebody (academia or industry) brainwashed them. I have concluded that education may in fact be either liberating or obstructive to the primal spirit's free expression. Institutions with higher prestige may be more likely to foster offspring with egos trained to outcompete the competition without consideration of social justice. This is only part of the issue.

Higher intelligence can easily discern wrong from right. However, behavior does not follow intelligence, it follows heart. Unfortunately, very intelligent people may have rotten hearts, and these people are dangerous to others. Thus, we should not uniformly rely on intelligence in driving higher education. The ego should be educated first by love, then by intelligence. The outcome of ego maturation should be liberation of intuition, with it's *a priori* knowledge of universal humanitarian principles such as justice and equality.

I live in the woods, not because it is fashionable and not only because others have described something dear there:

> I went to the woods because I wished to live deliberately, to front only the essential facts of life, and see if I could not learn what it had to teach, and not, when I came to die, discover that I had not lived. I did not wish to live what was not life, living is so dear; nor did I wish to practise resignation, unless it was quite necessary. I wanted to live deep and suck out all the marrow of life, to live so sturdily and Spartan-like as to put to rout all that was not life, to cut a broad swath and shave close, to drive life into a corner, and reduce it to its lowest terms.[5]

—Henry David Thoreau,
Walden: Or, Life in the Woods

I live in the woods because that is my home, where I learned that God is mystical and all of life is mystical as well, an extension of sublime intelligence and loving Nature (interdependent principles), and yes, we grow to

---

[5]   Henry David Thoreau *Walden* (State Street Press: New York, 2000) 105

know life better each day, hopefully, experiencing the glory through everyday occurrences.

In my experience, love is the key to life, and it is also the key to healthy-mind space. Mystics teach us to cultivate minds built for purity and simplicity, forever traveling inward to experience God in quietude on a personal level. We should desire to tame our egos, and our inquisitive minds, and also to become more loving so that we will be more lovable. I believe that taming one's ego is just one key to man's journey toward peace. I am less qualified to speak on the topic of the feminine ego, but I suspect, at the core, when stripped of societal cloaks, the human ego is consistent across genders. With a tame ego, man can properly love himself, and his neighbors as well, depending on how much he has to offer, and he also must make good choices to be able to discover his most beautiful life. Taming an ego allows one to become loving, and being a loving person is a wonderful destination, because then you are heavily lovable. I believe it is also wonderful to search for beauty in others once one finds true beauty in one's own self.

Nature and Religion

Nature is a convenient substrate for reflection on religion.

I suspect that birds, and perhaps many animals as well, might have very well-developed senses of religious intuition, albeit perhaps these senses function at different frequencies from the ones our consciousness(es) are used to. Humans, on the other hand, appear to be frequently lacking in intuition, in good sense, and even have trouble recognizing exactly what intuition is, because all they know clouds the eye of intuition, putting it to sleep with thoughts about information and knowledge and overly rigid belief in poorly defined thoughts and ideas gathered by distorting hijacked emotions. Antoine Artraub, a major figure of twentieth-century theater, used the word *antipoetry* to my liking. I believe he was talking about perverse intelligence when he wrote, "Like silent rage, the most terrible plague is the one that does not reveal its symptoms."[6] It is more or less my idea that some people cannot communicate with animals and birds because of learned patterns (antipoetry) that block their abilities to perceive. My evidence is that once the blockage is unlearned, in my case, I could communicate with nonhumans.

When the mind has been further cultivated by prayer and reverence, it becomes more useful than perhaps even the most educated of us can appreciate. The mind so cultivated is not only quiet; it is cool. Our minds are much cooler than we realize. When minds are cool, consciousness can hang out. Higher education helps keep all things balanced in that cultivated mind as well. Thus, higher education can be useful especially if one's mind is first cultivated by prayer.

The religious mind freely chooses to practice devotion, and through precise and fully committed exercise attains grace, which no longer requires intellect, nor persuasive argumentation, nor astute definition, to receive and achieve understanding of God's perfect love.

*We should be open to the possibility that God the Father wants us to come together and share our respective cultures, not to annihilate each other as the rumor has been. If God (the Father) had previously a violent side, perhaps it has mellowed. Perhaps we have mellowed His violence for Him.

As a final point, religion is a good thing when it keeps like-thinking minds together for the purpose of honoring God, and when it acts as a form of interpersonal abundance for many. The religious mind should also understand that what is needed next is a communication linkage among the various like-minded religious groups (that are users of God's mind) so that God's plan of blessing us with His knowledge can manifest more smoothly.

Against Corruption

I suspect the reason politicians treat us like children is because we spend so much time preferentially as machine minds. We ignore them (politicians), just when they need us to pay the most attention. How could they be so corrupt if we kept our eyes on them? Some of the most corrupt politicians are benefiting from lack of term limits in a very interesting respect. Because there are no congressional term limits, congressmen of outstanding power can survive incredible corruption exposure and still get reelected, perhaps because their precincts benefit from their corrupt behavior. People continue to elect corrupt politicians perhaps because it is beneficial to do this, but also because the process of electing leaders is potentially corrupt. The problem, of course, is that we all fall under the political authority of such corruption. Elected leaders support laws that protect the establishment. Through congresspeople's support of corrupt policy, they are attacking both our lives and our children. We need to protect our turf. We must battle and defeat corruption, by reformation of congress.

Against Violence

As a society, I believe we need to carefully define our interests. For example, bullying should be excluded from the list. We no longer need violence for revolution (the military can rest), and in fact violence won't work because we control the violence, at least the violent reaction. Terrorists play with us because we are programmed to respond in the direction they want. However, terrorists hate the establishment, and our violent response to terrorism is exactly what the establishment wants, so terrorism helps the establishment. Is it perhaps true that the establishment exists only because of conflict? If we stop conflict, the establishment (violent mindset) might die. If terrorists knew that they only help the establishment whenever they create violence, then they might stop that tactic. If we choose nonresponse, the establishment loses, yet one cannot exist in fear, and terrorism must be opposed. This will be difficult because the establishment and their media want violent response, perhaps need violent response.

We (let's be unanimous) want a nonviolent society. I firmly believe that it is unethical to sell arms to third parties who murder innocent victims. In my opinion, the global arms industry is guilty of multiple, countless acts of accessory to murder, and the entire industry should be sentenced to death. We need to inactivate the violent response capacity of the adolescent threats we now seem to know intimately, as if face-to-face, by listening to them seriously and negotiating with them. With determination, we might eventually end hostility on our planet. However, until we disarm those who bear aggressive adolescent hatred against us, we will continue to rely on our military to protect us, and we are grateful to them for their service. This contradiction arises by looking at the issue of two valid yet opposing perspectives.

It is easy to determine what is leading today's culture (materialism), but my dream is that we can collectively move toward education and away from consumerism, toward peace and harmony, oneness with Nature, and away from violent destruction. Hopefully, this present conversation will help with taking off the Band-Aid and jumping on the bandwagon. It would be liberating to have production and advertisement regulated so that toxins could be eliminated from our shopping cart. This could possibly happen someday. I believe that freedom will come when we no longer passively support toxic exploitative endeavors. Lying must stop, and murder must stop, and education must accelerate, because education works best in the absence of lies. As a first step, we need to sniff out the lies, then snuff them out.

Cold Blooded

Not all thoughts have feelings. Some are like plastic. Thoughts can be cold-blooded. I suppose some people might get pleasure from cold-blooded thoughts. Others, like myself, prefer humor, for example, which generally is of such intellectual force that even cold-blooded thinking is allowed to participate in the warmth of laughter good humor is capable of enticing.

On the social horizon, we need to take the capacity for violence away from those who make it their purpose to kill or terrorize others. The cold-blooded truth is that we can achieve this goal by electing problem solvers that are committed to ending violence rather than conventional politicians committed to economic concerns, because "GNP follows arms sales" as my wise old Ivy League economist friend told me. Likewise, we must stop the production of plastic, as it is toxic to the Earth, our primal habitat. Go ahead; blame plastics on us scientists. It is not a spiritual problem, because scientists are not spiritualists; they invented a birth control agent in the beginning, and then the birth control agent (artificial female hormone) was added to strengthen the plastic and make it flame-retardant, and its impact perhaps is not only pollution, undeniably nonbiodegradable pollution, but also premature puberty in females (it's a female hormone; the effect on males is unknown, but plastic is lethal to albatrosses as evidenced by avian necropsy studies). There is also the breast cancer epidemic, also in women, the cause of which might be environmental toxins, of which plastic is a major culprit (Americans reportedly throw out sixty million plastic bottles every day).

Blind consumption of products packaged in plastics is selfish, so slowing down is a great goal, even for those who might otherwise like plastic. You don't have to stop altogether. Some plastics have long service lives and are of high value, so don't dispose of them so readily if you in fact find that you need them every so often (like plastic shopping bags) and enjoy the convenience of their presence in your lives (like ice cube trays). However, if the desire is to give someone a nice toy, for example, and the toy has lots of plastic wrapping, the end result of buying the toy is support of the plastics industry and the continued toxification of Earth. If ego can recycle plastic, it can also refuse to buy excess plastic.

Recycling plastic must become an animalistic act. Yet, as long as we buy it, they will keep making it. We must kill the production of plastics by killing the market for plastics. We must make the manufacture of plastics illegal on Earth. That's cold-blooded thinking, from a scientist who cares.

Final Thoughts of a Mad Scientist

For any two brains, including right and left brains, to share time, there needs to be both emotional content and emotional control. This is not the same as emotional repression. The reason for this requirement that emotions be present is the fact that emotions open the brain, and thus expand available mind space (just like when we purge data from our hard drive to make room for apps to function). The effects of emotions on our brains are unbelievable! Surely some functions are inhibited, while many others, such as artistic and athletic endeavors, are enticed by emotion. For brains to share time in a productive manner, leading to understanding, there needs to be love, a positive emotion. Negative emotion does not work, as negativity resists expansion of mind space, perhaps as part of an innate defense mechanism. Yet such negativity can be skillfully converted into positivity, relaxing the mind and allowing it to open. If a mind were waiting for the correct time to open and someone tried to force his or her way in, negativity would be a good defense to keep it closed, that's for sure. When would the sense of vulnerability recognize the correct time? When the negativity (fear) is neutralized.

Because out of control thought fueled by emotion can lead to violence, many believe that emotion causes violence. Many fear emotion. Yet oftentimes violence is emotionless, cold-blooded, and calculated. For many, violence arouses emotion. This makes me wonder if something other than emotion causes violence, causes loss of emotional control.

We can speak to each other using the emotions, peacefully, when the psychology becomes quieted. We can pass our warm feeling to others via a gentle nod, for example, or a slight smile only when we are thoughtless. If we have thoughts, the receiver will receive the message that "I'm occupied," but not the warmth one might think is portrayed, unless we perhaps have highly persuasive body language as well.

Our bodies continue to talk to each other even when our minds are active in other ways, body language. This is usually not a problem if we are honest.

Most importantly, we need to be emotionally free because emotions are important means by which God touches us and enters our lives, and by which we touch others and enter their lives. People with desires to not think survive just fine. Billions and billions of thoughtless organisms share the Earth with us. Surely they exist. It is because we feel that we exist, and it is God's love that we truly feel once we get the truth straightened out.

But don't get me wrong. Thought has plenty of merit, especially loving thought.

The End